OLD DAMSON-FACE

L M

OLD DAMSON-FACE

Poems 1934 to 1974

Bernard Gutteridge

LONDON MAGAZINE EDITIONS LONDON
1975

For Lucy, Ann-Marie
and Cosima Gutteridge

Published by London Magazine Editions
30 Thurloe Place, London, S.W.7.
© Bernard Gutteridge 1975

SBN 904388 08 5

Some of these poems were printed in *Traveller's Eye*
(Routledge 1947). Others are previously unprinted;
the rest have appeared in *London Magazine*.

Designed and printed at
The Compton Press Ltd.
Compton Chamberlayne
Salisbury, Wiltshire

CONTENTS

Poems from 1946 onwards

RIM OF RED

"She rode a race on me," Jim chauffeur said.
"She took her specs off and her tits fair swung."

They were the days they bought french letters coiled
In mock cigarettes. "Bloody near drew it off

Of me." He and I lay naked beside the cold Test
And with affection he stroked his cock.

Nobody else on the river bank. "I'll get a horn
On if we don't go in again." I was ten.

"Those bleeding fish worth a thousand quid a mile a week."
With rushing weeds and cold that already hurt.

But often naked by rivers or seas I have
Remembered my idea of how her nose would bear

A rim of red from steel glasses, breasts like swings.
And confiding, white, hairy Jim, favouring his cock.

THE CHOUGHS

We said we would
See choughs together one day.

A cold-cold, gull-gull
Saltish cry; high stepped above

Black rocks these floating
Black sea-coast birds.

But how to know on Mizzen Head
That was the last day of our love?

They cry the heart down to
An echo that's not there;

We said we would
See choughs together one day.

IN PIMLICO

There you are sick in that bad room;
Your last life-and-death-line telephone
Sweating to take your grasp at any call.

Here's Ebury Fields where they buried then
The Plague dead. Our generation
Used to mass graves; waxed, hived bodies asprawl.

I walk in flight of your death, above
These abhorred bones: white, heaped mycelium.
No guts to make the sick telephone call.

AT THE LION (A SEQUENCE)

"I am prescribed unhappiness;
And that is why I drink it."

1.   TEARS, HEART

We alcoholics have a moist eye
For disaster, a bantam cock, a T.V.
Spectacular. Anything just above or below,

Above or below – only minutely –
Above or below our weeping point.
You must not think, "a tender heart".

Watch the eyes' webbed corners, skin
Like bird feet in mud under
Shifting water, moist, condensation.

"I'll cry my pathos after everything
(Go, dog and hunt it down!) that's
Simple or maudlin, rare, astringent."

Unleash the tears. They have their
Part to tell of what we are.
The heart dried out real tears past.

2. DOG-SITTER

I am her dog-sitter
He says and proves and pours.
Booze growls inside him:
Heel! Heel-tap! Hennessey!
Begs for doubles and applause.

Under his seat, the battered
Sealyham like his wife;
The lead creaks as he jerks its
Collar and tries to pretend
To pretend to strangle his life.

3. HIS OWN TABLE

The guest house, alcohol,
Where you stay and are stayed.
The drummer on the beach, the drum,
The sticks, the taps.
Old bruised legs along
The empty promenade.
Landlady of my gin!
O lodger whisky!

4. BOTTLE TOPS

Bottle tops fall always upside down.
Crown-corks they are called in the trade.
Foliated, crimped,
When done with there's a dent in them
Like all us gentlemen.

5. H. OBIT. 1973

I'd trade my whisper for a gin.
Shuffle the glass across the counter.
Drink's worth a take; drink is a move won

Only when the board is folded and all
Our pieces in the wooden box.
Slide it across, old opponent, I'll tell

You wanted to know.
Just that your attack was always great,
Your defence, weak. And that was how . . .

6. OLD DAMSON-FACE

My Bar, 'Good-morning' friend: damson-face.
My looking-glass of fractured capillaries
I shall hang up before me in a decade.
That puffed nose you own will be mine;
The hanging cheeks – such fritillaries –
Shaking, shaking, shaking like the wine.

When did you start? I know! Just before
You could ever stop. Your seismic mysteries
So many shakes to a glass or round called.
The marble clatter that glasses sing
Tucked in your rubrics and your histories
Shifting, shifting, shifting like each ring.

Old damson-face, my Bar, 'Good-morning' friend.
Move over. I have to place *my* orders now.
The brain gone, please; the next-but-nine-years round.
Smoke the lips; eyes, always, tears.
Into the purple, over the borders, now,
Waiting, waiting, waiting like the years.

A generation ago this wisp of tobacco moustache
Sold silk stockings door to door in Garden Cities
When front door bells all still went Ping!
Not La-di-da-di-carillon-di-da!

He's like the horn on a bull-nose Morris that
Wouldn't stop. His foot is still inside the door,
Still plugging *Num*. His bar side reminiscing
Demands the answer yes, provokes the no.

Fishpaste sandwiches, a cup of tea and a swift
Bit of crumpet, boy, were occupational twists.
The Bar is all one room now; there's no Saloon;
Crossed knees are public, too-young now, and nylon.

There is no Mild. All's Keg. The travelling salesmen
Sport Zodiacs, Gin-and-Tonics. He would never ever
He says have put on a striped shirt and a slogan topper
To be a Detergent Man with fivers in Housing Centres.

8. MY LIFE

She nags her life out of me.
Over my whisky I see the poor sod run
Shouting *bitch* over its shoulder.

And here she comes back out of the Ladies,
Dribbling it back at me,
Preparing to shoot.

FROM MOTHER GOOSE (A SEQUENCE)

1.

Let's to bed said Sleepy Head
Tarry a while said Slow
Put on the pan said Greedy Nan
We'll sup before we go.

When you're young it's Sleepy Head
Middle-aged it's Slow
But if you're old it's Greedy Nan
We'll suck before we go.

2. THE FARMER'S WIFE'S MOUSE

Smell the bait, blind snuffle-face;
Touch the poised place.
Then with a slow, smooth, soft snap –
In my trap!

3. FAIRY TALE REVERSED

Yes said the Shepherdess lying with the Prince
I'll have your virginity for the price of a quince
And put it in slowly and promise not to wince.

In slipped the Prince's tool, a soft hard hot rod
O sighed the Shepherdess I've got me a Mod-God
My eyes in the heavens and my bum on a moss sod.

Then as his weapon magicked Gog and Magog
It turned from its living blood to an ice dead elm log
And his hands on her breasts were the flippers of a Frog.

4. DAUGHTER GOOSE

Goosed on the escalator,
goosed on the moving stairs,
a rushtime mini
get-together
('he tweaked my hairs').

It makes you take 'Goosey-goosey-gander
whither did you wander'
seriously, eh old comrade,
old researcher?

And what of 'old man by his legs'
and 'threw him down the stairs'?
Groping in the lady's feathered
chamber at our age!

5. HANS

His hands blubbering away
In the empty oak chest,
Victim of a fairy tale,
Waves each cropped wrist.

He can't even have his
Fingerprints back,
The sucked wart on the thumb
Or his lifeline back.

But tomorrow they'll
Prop up his glass of gin,
The weepy hands. They'll gristle
Back again.

Do quite remember
He believed the promise,
Turned the key quickly,
Dipped in his hands.

FLIERS

The twilight slings bats
between shadow and shadow,
warm black gristle
living on smoke

The floating gibbons in
their penthouse
iron square
eating up air.

Ravens in black pairs
beat up the mountain face,
cough darkness over the sea.

HEDGEHOG

Among seedlings, not balled
As they usually are if a dog
Noses them out of their dark.
Usually you see them at night

Or in day, dead on a road.
But squat down, open, jerking
Its sweat-wet bristles like a shirt
Or skin to be rid of.

We guessed the hedgehog was dying,
Hoped it was parturition.
It ate bread-and-milk,
Heaved on tried-for journeys.

The child who found it took
Her unspiky ball away to bounce.
Frightened? Yes. Avoiding death's
Movements? Yes. Or birth's.

PRIVATE

Not just the whole face mutinous;
The small thin body shrinks into a
Muttering of local malice.
Witch. Cat. Black. Shrew.
A private demonology of fur
Rubbed backwards, words twisted.

WHAT BECAME OF JIM HAWKINS?

Squire now; sonless heir to sonless
Kind old amateur buccaneer.
'I believe in God' I tell my
Vicar and my congregation.
Wonder in what barrel of apples
That lie goes remarked.

Twigs knock blindly my windowpanes.
Winter: blind cold Pew tapping his
Beat towards death under horseshoes.
Summer: a loved, feared one's dot-and-carry.
Ashplant, oakleg – I grow them all.
The birds cry 'Pieces of Eight'.

Only Doctor Livesay would have known
(Would have no reek of the Treasure),
Known too when I slop my port
Israel Hands's blown blood I suck.
Forecast to a boy of fourteen
Careened from love or lust forever.

OLD ELMS

(In Memoriam Perce and Dick)

A winter deep-breathing for oak and ash; holly
   Warms up for Christmas.
But oh they die, these old ones
   They warned us with their
Yellow leaves all summer.

In the autumn we felled and burned
   Our elms. Churchyard
Yews took to their roots some old, younger
   Parishioners; cradled
Again under the stretched downs.

What double-Dutch, Dutch-courage bug
   Gets through my bark one day
I won't ever know. But I know I won't
   Come down with such a crash –
Leave evermore a blue sky space
Or evict a green woodpecker.

NOVEMBER

Rake up the leaves
Scarify the grass.
Autumn and winter now
Take much of your time.
You are tidying up
Your life my only
Life-long friend
That's left to me now.
Father and mother, uncles,
Aunts. Dead the vine
In the greenhouse.
The walnut tree down.
And I don't count
The flint of an old house.

THUMB

We don't like you, we four.
You have a different name.
You thumb things.
You have prints.
You stamp. We love.

STOWAWAY

Look at the young man, there,
That one, good with the bridesmaids
And attentive in his simple way
With the bride,
And the champagne

Notice the young lady breaking
The bottle, naming the ship Venture.
Remember that at each wedding,
Each launching,
Mutiny is the first stowaway.

Poems between 1934 and 1938

MAN INTO A CHURCHYARD

He comes unknown and heard and stands there.
Breathes there hardly and hands grip
Flesh and walking stick. Skips over mounds
To land flat footed in a bowl of roses.

Flicks at the crazy gravestones
Spitting loud desires wood crosses for himself:
Heaves them up with laughter to hang them,
Dangling on the atheist's fig tree.

Handsprings through the open door,
Signs with a swastika on the visitors' book
With a pansy in his buttonhole.

IN A CONVEX MIRROR

Stare where the colours
Sit in the splintered curtain
And wide room expands itself from the centre
Effacing the walls as uncertain,
Unable to climb in the course
Of the convex glass.

And people come in and out and do not wait,
And children sometimes cry or stay good.
The outside comes past the great
Window though, and stays in the mirror for days.

With head grown enormous and eyes with seeing far
Imagine a finer wood beyond this wood, and another
Finer still: as seen from clouds or mirrored down
Shaftings of sun and passing like a frown.
Think of our hopes for money, little loves,
Visiting distant friends and health and far longer lives.

Until we must draw the curtain, wait for tea,
Turn on the electric light, the sudden eye.
Now clip all the windows and walk in the lanes,
Finger the wheat, examine the evening sky,
Or talk of what our paper well explains.

PARABLE

You who glint enviously from the hard-baked towns
And imagine feathered horses that impalpably lead,
Turning earth over downs, and think cosily of farmhouse fires
With fresh bread and the comforting dialect of the wind,
Should know you watch from the wrong side of the screen.

This is no countryside of the provident ego
Reflected in the windows of author's country cottages,
But more a mass than ever of the huddled sheep
Of winter woods lying under the seduction of snow,
The farmers scraping like robins for their food.

The freedom here is the truth of the parable –
While the hard legs of the paralytic
Cannot move in the soft bed by any effort of will
He is mocked painfully by lightness of the nurse's hands
Treading their way over his parched thighs.

HOLDERNESS

Here on this Yorkshire lawn with the smell of cut grass
And the loose wire window flapping in the pantry,
 I remember in the distance
 The correction of silence,
 A childhood of hope and chance.

Along the borders the delphiniums and lupins flowering;
The fig tree dark against the wall; the cautious, brown
 Intrusion of hens; the cold
 Wood of the chair, and old
 Sounds and hedges that build

Especially these twenty acres into an ivory tower
As real as that Napoleonic tower of scarlet brick
 Beyond the road, that guards
 This line of coast; its stairs
 Rotting, dirtied by birds.

Eastward the diminution of hay or unripe corn
Down to the cliff's edge but growing thin and weak
 Where the few bathers walk
 And the sandy fields look
 Poor for the farmer's luck.

Where the sea holds out its bay like a green carafe
Into the pincers of the sand and the red sticky clay,
 Here are the wiry grasses,
 The dry extravagant dunes
 That no water washes.

Insulated by thatched north walls, the yellow house
Devotes its silhouette to the bank of elms,
 Holding the marks of living
 Against the dark green ring
 And the rooks cawing.

Antirrhinums in blue bowls, oil paintings of hunters
With their badly drawn sharp intelligent faces, their windowless stalls;
    And the curtains like lids
    Shading the polished boards
    And carpets in dark bands.

Yes, here where the massive barometers and clocks and guns
And the oak chests seem exactly like my grandfather,
    I feel myself secure
    Against any real desire
    And against you, my dear.

With your smart expensive clothes and easily laddered stockings,
Your painted finger-nails and golden hanging hair,
    Your lightly accepted
    Love might be disproved,
    Your position removed

As easily as any Mrs. Sinkin's pink
Is caught up in the lawn-mower's whirling knives:
    All of you that I know
    Be alien, would grow
    Diffident, awkward, slow.

Your fascinating smile and the simple bodily grace you give,
Your platter of proffered love and childish greed;
    All of you that I hold
    Change from its glinting gold
    As the sunflowers fold.

Nettles and laurels in the derelict Quaker chapel;
The doctor's wife on the beach in a yellow costume;
    And the chevroned sands;
    The doctor's regular rounds,
    Always keeping in bounds.

The strange nyctalopy of memory when the house
Is locked and bolted; my grandfather might be alive,
　　Inside with whisky and cards.
　　The mourning eyes of shutters
　　Plausible with their blank stares

That nightly shut out the hesitating swoops of bats
And the tramp-like snores of the young owls. But to-day
　　It is afternoon, and these
　　Memories fade with the years
　　And they do not appease.

So I sit comfortably among the straight white lines,
The precise arrangements of eating, drinking and sleeping,
　　Lounge under a hot sun
　　With no day's work done,
　　Nothing attempted or done.

HOME REVISITED

Now that I go there as a visitor,
To the end of the short lane,
And pass the rockery with a stranger
Walk, I can recall his death again.

Birth and death identically change
While the house remains the same;
Grow from a boyhood's sword-sharp lunge
Of fear and love to an imagist's game.

Birth as the red ribboning of a cot,
An unknown nurse in a rage;
As the seven swallows that sit
Dropping their pellets on the saxifrage

That wags its racket seed pods in the wind
Rotting brownly from the centre;
The doctor's shadow on the blind
Spring, summer, autumn or winter.

Death as my walking past this empty shell:
The fixed memory of life
Ceasing like echoes in a well
Beyond the last ripple of short grief.

Death as a circle of nettles where the hut
Turned the patient to the wind.
That wind has taken seeds and set
Dock leaves' tusk roots into the heavy ground.

Or as the untidy nests the starlings build
To forever leave or enter;
The doctor's shadow on the blind
Spring, summer, autumn or winter.

PLYMOUTH HOE: MIST

Over the harbour every minute light
Becomes a Star. Darkness as suave and calm
Engrafts all but the searchlight's smoothing beams,
Squared on the water that the seaplanes sight.

Islanded in her bedroom the sad lover
Divines her sensual images of war.
Gershwin, Berlin: the deceptive axiom
Of dance slurs from the gliding ballroom floor.

The rocks and the destroyers threaten harm;
The thought of mist evokes its taunting dreams
Of smothering sheets; the pinnaces withdraw
Beneath the breakwater's concreted arm.

As easy for gulls the fairway seems,
Floodlit for entering planes; the gawky town
Lies its enormous shadow on the shore;
Against pier stanchions the tide twists and creams.

But the breeze drops. The streamers settle down;
And for the seaplanes the obscuring light
Repeats the rumour from the murdering moor.
Under the sea of mist the pylons drown.

Poems between 1939 and 1945

IN SEPTEMBER 1939

The last war was my favourite picture story.
Illustrated London News bound in the study;
The German bayonet we believed still bloody

But was just rusty. Privacy of death.
My uncle's uniform meant more than glory;
Surprise that grief should be so transitory . . .

All the predictions of adolescence had
Disposed of glory in their realist path:
There'd be no need to duck and hold your breath.

Yet from the blacked-out window death still seems
Private, not an affair that's shared by all
The distant people, the flats, the Town Hall.

But some remember Spain and the black spots
They shouted "Bombers" at. That memory screams
That we know as a film or in bad dreams.

Fear will alight on each like a dunce's cap
Or an unguessed disease unless death drops
Quicker than the sirens or the traffic stops.

ROUGH SHOOT AT GALASHIELS

Bobbing like a drifter's strung-out line of floats
Ten guns worry the game through coppices
And slapping wet leaves of roots. Only cocks are shot.

Gamekeepers in fawn leggings; a red
Setter in a black hedge; mist of smoke from a barrel;
As still as the Tweed water that lies like lead.

Flaxen haystacks on the treacle plough;
Woodcutters' stubble of trees on Gala Hill –
Axes stopped, woods spoiled of their echoes now.

I wonder what gaps war's guns will hack
About this linked party of my friends.
So death like green seas obliterated one black

Speck in the line, sinking for ever.
And here if one of us lay below the sea of leaves
The others might forget he had been there, and never

Notice; go on forward again, the Tweed still,
The red setter still; the hare crash helplessly
From the black mouths of the guns' will.

SUNDAY PROMENADE: ANTSIRANE

Big bummed and bubbed
The bibis walk down to the Joffre memorial:
Native police white clubbed
And Catholic priests censorial.
All the British soldiery there
Taking it in with a bold stare;
Black bottoms through chiffon gleaming,
Sunlight streaming
And the come-hither air.

Away they go!
The bibis stroll back up the Rue Colbert;
Bougainvillaeas glow
Their purple bloom about the air.
British soldiery gay as a lark
Wink at each other, all remark
Black posteriors blandly weaving,
Sunlight leaving
All the fun of the dark.

PATROL: BOUNAMARY

Beyond the white dust flushed by the carriers
A scena of mangrove and sea:
Ten small figures running stumbling over the hill,
Our bullets yelping after like harriers
Keen on a kill.

And that was all the enemy's resistance.
The pot-bellied children fondled
Tommy guns and Brens, brought bananas; stared.
The chalk road gashed into the distance,
The sea glared.

The men swam idly all the afternoon,
Beech leaves on the brilliant water;
The tide dropped; stems of the mangroves shiny and seal black
Lifted tight green sheaves from the lagoon;
The horizon went slack

With orange sunset slipping into the sea.
Sentries were detailed and posted.
Night followed the shadows, snakes of fire leapt
Where the men smoked and brewed their tea,
Gossiped and slept.

And in the policeman's house I slowly sipped
The poisonous rhum with some alarm;
Admired a photo of De Gaulle, laboured: "Oui,
Paris avec les Boches, Madame,
Ce n'est pas Paris".

TANANARIVE

Hills blossom in small red houses; the palace
Governs like an implacable queen her plains
And lazing people. The children play like ducklings.
All are so happy but nothing here seems clean
Except the gull-like washing and white arum lilies.

We take over the bars and speak English arrogantly,
Stare at the pigeon-crouching French whose faces
Speak with their voices. Rhum, citron and orange pressé:
And sly, beautiful soignée women take
No notice at all of our caps and Sam Brownes.

Flags are saluted everywhere. Above the dusty street
High in the lilac trees we see from the verandah
The ice-like stillness of encircling ricefields, greenly glinting;
Pousse-pousse boys jolt past like broken toys
And above us all the time frowns the forbidding palace.

Some of it is quite lovely. Down in the market-place
An acre of red and white carnations, a moving scent of cloves,
And girls like Hedy dressed in Gauguin colours
Slipping among the striding, pavement-ringing soldiers,
And subtle, ageless children more wicked than any pirate.

Till night holds all its treacheries cupped like a black breast
With light in the town its sensuous, desirous smile.
All over the small hills depart the ambushing steps
That crumble and snare; and in the drifting gloom
The velvet stab of pleasure that pushes to the heart.

BURMA DIARY

1. ARAKAN

Up to the hard sky, down to the burnt fields
Of paddy, lunge the terrible hills
Spined with unlovely trees and scrub,
   Scratched with red gravel rash.

Dust is harsh on dry skins; grass cuts like wire,
Tendrils in the jungle hang as traps
Set with a grenade. Down off the watershed
   We wait the sly enemy,

His tough, short smelly body like a stump
Grown in the scarious chaungs. Death
Ambushes among the spiked bamboos,
   Barbed behind glossy leaves.

So when I heard these last two afternoons
My friend, a poet, had died on the Goppe Pass;
Another, my dearest friend, next day was killed
   Leading his company –

And looking Eastwards to the Mayu Range,
Its barren hulk all burned up in the heat,
Somehow it was quite expected; and I write
   These arid lines, alive myself,

For the actual and real is Burma. Alun and Amyas
Will never return through the streams and jungle,
Their physical part of the pattern is ended.
   The soft Welsh voice

Telling a story in French in an Indian garden
By scarlet flowers. Huge Amyas playing rugger
Or walking at my side in Christmas sunshine
   Saying, "This is being alive".

46

All that remains are the frailest moments
Between two bursts: minute that is a friend gone,
That is the twist of terror, a ricochet,
  A cloud, a sampan sinking.

A prisoner on a brown stretcher among grey stones;
Fawn bamboo feathers shuffle up the hills
Under the breeze of the watercourse. His blood
  Reddens the white bandage.

His voice is a thin mowing to the brisk
Interpreter; our soldiers staring; above
And around quick rattles from Brens and rifles
  And suddenly like splinters

The bullets among us whistling going Smack!
And chipping the stones; We on our bellies again,
The black hair of the prisoner beside me,
  Eyelids falling with pain.

Or the village of Maungdaw lying dead
By the Naf River. The yellow blasted huts
Collapsed among their gangling bamboo stilts,
  Black ashes and scorched grass.

Dust is the blanch of death upon the plain
And shrouds the carriers and men and guns.
All you follow are cinnamon drifting clouds
  That sway along the roads.

Seven streamers of gold are Sherman tanks –
The Dragoons moving in on Buthidaung –
Kalapanzin River sinewy, silver flat
  In squares and rectangles of fields.

The prisoner wears a cherry blossom badge, *Sakurai Heidan.*
We probe into his other life: his letters from home
And photographs; the poetry he wrote
    Under the trees at Maymyo.

"Even the fragrance of the cigarette I smoke
Brings back memories of my cherished home. Who is this man
Who has come to this land? No one but I
    Whose bones are to remain."

2. HOPIN

These slant-eyed, untrustworthy Burmans ploughed
This paddy until from the Western hills
To the quick Namkwin chaung the valley entire
    Was planned to its neat squares.

In the green villages they climbed up ladders
And slept above the floods: their extravagance
A silken longyi, and as at Hopin,
    The blessing of the Buddha

Whose infinite peace is changeless as the rim
Of violet hills. The gold-painted great God
Is enshrined in coloured glass the pattern of paddy,
    In squares and triangles,

But blue, purple and crimson, green and diamond.
A battalion of soldiers is living there to-day
Patrolling the overgrown fields, happy to find
    Roses among the sighing bamboos,

Paying fabulous prices for hens, bathing naked
In the icy water, fit and somehow happy.
And coming from the hills, the villagers
    With rickety babies

And horrible jungle sores along their legs
For once sense friendliness: they grasp at smiles
As their own children grab at sardines and chocolate –
    Something unknown before.

3. NAMMA

Everything must, of course, exist for people.
For example, at Namma the Chinese colony
With drabbish, flat-chested women, so alien
    To our China of blossom,

And hoary, sly old men and flash, slick dirty youths –
The entire set-up redeemed only by children
In chiffon skirts, with dusty tawny bodies,
    Attractively shy or pert.

They all live in some fifty bamboo huts
That smell of sewers and manure or duck ponds.
In and out waddle plump ducks, spindly hens
    Or snorting black pigs.

Why cannot the sun and squalor, you think,
Deflower this green bush of its huge magenta blooms
Or blister the jasmine? Because they exist
    Here only, in the compound,

As do the children, for the eternal people.
They stand, slink-eyed and shady in the dung
To bargain their knowledge or their fowls:
    The inhabitants, the people.

Each soldier as he passes looks at their breasts
Laced tightly in childlike bodices (in Northern Burma, the full
Breasts of the Indian women are unfashionable),
    And lets his glance run

Over the swaying hips to their hard ugly feet.
They come to our small market with eggs for salt.
Yesterday there was one girl dressed in crimson
    Who lolled with a whore's walk

And plucked a flower with a sharp pull and jerk
So that her breast came free from her clothes –
As she intended – and at the soldiers' whistle
    Pretended to be shy.

But most are prim as they follow their bullock carts
And crossing the Namkwin Pul avert their eyes
For standing in the pink sunset that glides
    Along the kine grass spears

Knee high in the water the soldiers soap their thighs
And crack their bawdy jokes, brown to the waist.
And gleaming white bottoms – a hundred of them –
    Shock the Burmese lasses.

5. ASUGYI

Among hibiscus and papaia trees
The sugar-white pagoda points its thin
And branch-like iron spire above the palms
    Sharp at the brilliant sky.

Mia Maw and Tin Shwe build their private gold
Pagodas from the Shweli mud: their model
Swaying with trees in the black green water.
    Egrets like flowers stand.

The full-robed pongyi meditates on grace,
Blankets, his rice, the brinjal seeds, the Lord
Who is the pongyi chaung and palisade
    And all the sandy earth.

Here stepping as slowly as meditation
Baw Thaw the builder of this new pagoda comes;
Noiseless, drifts on the ground to gaze again
    At his white solemn gift.

Its eight bronze bells each with a leaf to catch
The smallest breeze and change it to a blessing
Soon will be green with verdigris and age,
    And the white stone dulled

With bronze green mosses darkened by monsoons.
The cluster of bricks that is his pledge for life,
Tin Shwe and Mia Maw to be grown old as him
    And he, having gained merit

Will be younger than them and gaze perhaps
On this stone shaded old, as a better man,
His spirit moving in a prosperous trader,
    A richer man.

But now transcending future the white spire,
The snowdrop egrets on the shadowed sand,
The full white clouds, all pierce like striking bells
    The green of prayer and peace.

6. MYITSON. THE SENTRY

This moonlight scans the river to its banks.
But there the gloss is broken into shadows.
Silence consumes the hollow heart of jungle.
 Movement and noise lie there

Folded by sleep and held by sharp nerves still.
Muscles like springs shudder beneath your skin.
Noise: the ripples, the croak of leaves, the bird,
 Jolt like a burn.

The prayer is: grant us no noise or movement.
Let the moon soothe the slipping water by
And no quick gasp to drum along the veins
 And drown the temples with fear.

THE PUPPETS AT THE WINTER PALACE, MONGMIT

The puppets that the children always left sprawling
With pink, branchlike legs and golden sneering faces –
Their dresses touched with fire – have bright, elaborate sequins.
One grows a cock's green head out of a man's body;
One screams in fear as he sees the black skies falling.
Under the charred nursery floor are: a splintered leg
With blue and silver foot; a hand; a thigh; torn trousers.
Before they left the children had set them brawling.

Now we with parachute cords get their thin legs dangling
Once more. After the time the enemy from the Monglong
    ranges
Had sent the children away, they lay and were bombed and
    burned

Only five puppets entire among twisted and shattered bodies.
They hint with their crooked jumps at the string's wangling –
As they once more jerk into a mockery of the fascinating evenings
Before the nursery burned – when often the man with muscular
    fingers
Set them to dance for the children, who laughed at their foolish
    jangling.

THE ENEMY DEAD

The dead are always searched.
It's not a man, the blood-soaked
Mess of rice and flesh and bones
Whose pockets you flip open;
And these belongings are only
The counterpart to scattered ball
Or the abandoned rifle.

Yet later the man lives.
His postcard of a light blue
Donkey and sandy minarets
Reveals a man at last.
"Object – the panther mountains!
Two – a tired soldier of Kiku!
Three – my sister the bamboo sigh!"

Then again the man dies.
And only what he has seen
And felt, loved and feared
Stays as a hill, a soldier, a girl:
Are printed in the skeleton
Whose white bones divide and float away
Like nervous birds in the sky.

GOLD MOHAR

A dark green lawn, a swathe
Of luteous bloom yet lingers.
And then this silver nicety
Of accurate trembling fingers.
The old tree with a lovely name
Graceful as its poised branches,
Old arms reaching to finicky twigs
The wind collects and launches,
A thin fern-like periphery.

You dead, my friends, still stay
Like this exquisite tree
My eyes must leave, heraldic
Flowering I will not see
Scald in April with crimson
Showers of petals. Then lie
There among its roots and blossom.
Your graces to the moonstone sky
It will yearly repay.

MANDALAY

Jumping like shrimps, clusters of thin brown children
Quarter the road, chucking bully tins of water
At every giggling, shrieking son and daughter.
It is the Water Festival. But the older people
Lack laughter and energy to crush these crippling years;
Lassitude more expressive now than tears.

The main road has been cleared but no one
Can hide the houses. For each roof is disaster,
The gimcrack walls grey-scarred in coloured plaster.
Pantheons of whitewashed Buddhas gleam in sunshine,
Stolid among the weeds of a stonemason's garden
Touched brown on thighs where swaying seed-pods harden.

Half of a smashed temple contains the crumbling
Remains of another Buddha. Splintered gewgaws
Of gods and devils among which young whores
Ruled by a sharp dark pimp in a brown trilby
Wait the same custom Japs had provided there,
Too tired to coax to life, drabs with greasy hair.

Sometimes the river or trees break through the streets;
Fleshy dollops of mangoes, light green jade,
Hang among dark laurel-like leaves. In shade,
A yellow pi dog scuttles among the bones
Of a dead bullock, looks out timid and mean
Through a cage of ribs the sun burned clean.

The tinsel petalled waves of Bougainvillaea
Lunge purple and scarlet their abandoned heaviness
Over frail bamboo huts. A mincing dancer dances
Bizarre in asters, his face a godlike white,
Blessing the peace of water and the rain's pity
Among the dark cowed people of a ruined city.

SHILLONG

I crowd all earth into a traveller's eye
Fragment by fragment. Only he
Can see the withering scar or sublime flower
For the first time joined in his own hour.

The market strewn with gutted fish; and fruit
Spewed open for the kites; the cries
And foul and sultry smell. A revered priest
Stooping in ashes; the greatest, the least.

Testing North towards Tibet the cold
Austere horizon of coarse green pines
Holds trapped the waterfall. The wide sky throws
White clouds towards the annihilating snows.

JOHANNESBURG

Gold smothers Johannesburg. Everthing –
Whisky and sun and dust and clouds – is gold.
The gold slag heaps are back-scene mountains
Encircling now this racecourse and its crowd.
Jacaranda trees blaze bright blue lanterns, colour

Caresses colour, violet with orange sleeves, striped cap;
Greys, chestnuts, pink tickets in lapels;
Buttercup golden jacket holds a minute jockey.
Slender girls enchant their rainbow dresses.
Then the white tapes fly and the line flames

And twenty horses batter down the straight.
Oh gold wins always by a length
Among the green trees pulling to a canter;
Walk back among the gardens of the paddock,
On the gay silks the gold sun's friendly banter.

BOMBAY

In Hornby Road and the Yacht Club, Bombay
Shines on as brightly as a playing card
Where still the Europeans boss and play:
Kings and Queens slightly part-worn, fit to discard.

Pavements are stippled with people. Jacks
Have fun as in Brighton shiny with bounders.
The Taj gives them its icy gins, almonds and snacks.
Along the grey edge of the sea the harbour flounders,

A dead forest of masts flowering in shifting gulls.
Slow sails on the water, tall sea lilies fawn,
The cricket ground tries to defeat the ocean and lulls
With pink and white deck chairs and strawberries on the green lawn.

Like any great city until the web of noises weaves
About you and holds you. The threatening noises in the street:
That dissonant horny quack of dry leaves;
And shuffle of bare feet on burning concrete.

The spying rustle of noise the white clothes –
Saris and dhotis – shake across a room.
Head turning hiss and grunt of a man who loathes
Our race and shows it. Drums in the small temples like doom

All night, as, bound Eastwards for the war,
The open casual West a memory growing less,
We move into the dark and sense once more
This sinister city uncoil its venomed softness.